NAPOLEON

A Life From Beginning To End

BY

Henry Freeman

Table of Contents

Introduction

The Little Corporal

Napoleon has always been a controversial figure. For some he was a clear enemy of the world, a kind of early prototype of the fascism that we saw in Germany, Italy, and Japan in the 20th century. But for others this couldn't be further from the case; for many of the French in particular, Napoleon is still viewed as a kind of national hero. Interestingly enough, the man who is often lauded as either the great French hero or the despicable French tyrant, wasn't even French - he was Corsican.

The man we know as Napoleon Bonaparte was born on the island of Corsica, in the Mediterranean city of Ajaccio. The son of a lawyer named Carlo Buonaparte, his father was originally a rebel that fought for the independence of Corsica from the French throne. Being a rebel among rebels, Carlo was one of many Corsican patriots with a long history of fighting for Corsican independence. Even before the French annexation of the island, Corsica was engaged in bitter struggle with another Mediterranean power; the Republic of Genoa.

With centuries of freedom fighting you could say that revolution was in the Bonaparte blood. Carlo like so many of his predecessors was a headstrong and vigorous fighter for the liberty of his people, but even he was eventually persuaded to lay down his arms in exchange for the perks and privilege his family would be given once they were guaranteed entry into the French nobility.

Carlo, whose vocation had never been secure in a Corsican economy that had been shattered over several decades of war, still suffered financially after the French annexation, but being lumped in with the French elite allowed him to send his son to the most prestigious schools. There, Napoleon would rub elbows with the rest of the French elite. This was how the Italian Napoleon was uprooted from Corsica at the age of 9 and sent to the mainland of France. In 1779 Napoleon was enrolled in the prestigious military school at the College of Brienne.

For the most part, in his early years Napoleon was received with a mixture of both warmth and ridicule. He was often made fun of for his still fairly thick Corsican accent and he was usually seen as more of a bookworm than someone who was ready to be socially inclined. It was here that Napoleon had received the infamous nickname, "Little Corporal", which was largely a sarcastic reference to his studiousness and serious demeanor.

All of his studying would eventually pay off however, leading to his early graduation from school at 16 and deployment to an artillery unit in Valence, where he would serve as one of the youngest officers. This marked the beginning of his lifelong fascination with the advancement of French munitions. It was here, surrounded by the things that he loved most, that Napoleon Bonaparte first began to make a name for himself and although young in age and short in stature, he was never short on enthusiasm.

His unbridled ambition was cut short however when he received word of his father's sudden death in 1786, an event which suddenly thrust the young Napoleon into the position of head of the household for his family in Corsica. Normally this role would have been placed on the eldest son, but Napoleon's brother Joseph was unemployed at the time. As a military officer, Napoleon was the only one with an income, so it was up to him to support his widowed mother and his siblings, causing him to travel back and forth between this Corsica and the French mainland for the next few years.

Despite this extra hardship, at this point in time the Little Corporal was a very ambitious young man, and by all accounts doing very well, although he was still somewhat limited by his Corsican heritage. In the pre-revolutionary system of the French Monarchy merit could only take you so far, and if you weren't born into the right family with all the prestige of the social elite, no matter how qualified you were you would invariably find yourself at a dead end.

But in 1789 the entire social structure of France would be turned upside down. Where you were born would suddenly be the least of people's concerns. French society was about to be shaken to its core, as the first fruits of the Enlightenment would take shape in Paris. There were a lot of ingredients that led to the complete overhaul of French society, and it is an intriguing fact to note that before ideas of enlightened revolution even reached the ears of partisans in France, the seeds of the French Revolution were actually sown in the Revolution of another country across the Atlantic: the United States.

Ironically enough, while the last French monarch Louis XVI did not support the ideals of democracy and liberty in his own country, he did seek to support them in the Americas. The main impetus in the French king's support of the American colonists wasn't necessarily because he supported the political system they espoused; it was more an effort to hurt his country's arch rival England.

However, in trying to weaken his enemy by supporting America, Louis XVI drained the French coffers dry. While his support was an integral part of the success in the American Revolution it left France completely broke, and yes, ironically enough, the brain drain that the King initiated is what sparked the French Revolution – which would lead to Louis' ultimate overthrow and demise.

From the storming of the Bastille to the Reign of Terror, Napoleon was an ardent supporter of the Revolution. Aligning himself early on with the Jacobins, Napoleon was a pragmatic realist. While he didn't agree with everything that the Jacobins represented, in this arm of the revolution he saw the potential for a strong centralized government that would be able to deal decisively with any issues facing the republic.

More importantly, Napoleon wanted to be on what he viewed as the "winning side", as he demonstrated in a letter to his brother when he wrote in shrewdly rational, Napoleonic fashion: "Since one must choose sides, one might as well choose the side that is victorious, the side which devastates, loots, and burns. Considering the alternative, it is better to eat than be eaten." And so implementing his own version of the adage, "If you can't beat them, join them," Napoleon was ready to cast his lot with the true winners of the revolution.

Napoleon positioned himself right in the middle of Jacobin affairs and was rewarded with the task of organizing and supervising elections for the local Jacobin governance of his native Corsica. It was here however that Napoleon faced stiff opposition from his own father's former compatriots, the Corsican independence fighters. Leading this charge was Pascuale Paoli, a former colleague of Napoleon's own father, and now governor of Corsica.

The faction that supported Paoli threatened Napoleon's ambition and Paoli's campaign against Bonaparte ended with the Corsican assembly condemning him as a traitor. His home was then ransacked, and in October of 1792 Napoleon and his family were forced to flee the island. As chaotic as his departure was, when Napoleon arrived back to France he found it to be in even more chaos, with the Reign of Terror from the revolutionaries in full force.

Even so, Napoleon, the loyal soldier of the revolution, worked to embark upon the beginning of his legacy as a great peacemaker and managed to help maintain some vestige of solidarity with the men under his charge during this adversity. This was a solidarity that was sorely needed in the country in the spring of 1794 when an expeditionary force of British, Austrian, and Spanish troops landed in southern France, occupying Toulon and threatening to push on further in the mainland. It was here that the young Captain Bonaparte found his true call to glory.

After gaining the support of Augustin Robespierre—the younger brother of Maximillien Robespierre, the head the infamous revolutionary body of the "Comite De Salut Public" (Committee of Public safety)—Napoleon was soon once again hand picked for favor. And when General Dinmartin was seriously injured in battle, it was the 24 year old Napoleon who this revolutionary consul turned to.

Already a trained artillery specialist, Napoleon was given full charge of the French artillery. Napoleon then led the charge to victory and scored a stunning success in the battle of Toulon. Unfortunately for Bonaparte the deck was stacked against him; soon after his great victory in battle, his benefactors the Jacobins were thrown out of power. It was here that Napoleon learned a very valuable lesson: loyalty to one's superiors only went so far, and even military victory was nothing in the face of political defeat.

Now that the Jacobins had been dismissed from their position as the ruling political class, Napoleon found himself not being hailed a hero but thrown in prison. The reasons for this confinement were purely political, based upon suspicions that were created due to Napoleon's endorsement by the just recently condemned Jacobins and their leader Maximilien Robespierre – a man who had himself just been subjected to the guillotine immediately before Napoleon's imprisonment.

Napoleon's consequent incarceration was simply a result of the fickle winds of fate during the turbulent times of the French Revolution. These winds were constantly changing direction and in such a volatile environment; one could find himself either being buffeted to the heights of victory or blown down into chasms of defeat at just a moment's notice.

Napoleon was soon cleared of charges, but to his great despair he was ordered to surrender his generalship and retire from the military outright. However, those turbulent winds of fate would change once again, largely due to the fact that there was a severe lack of able bodied and minded commanders, thanks to the effectiveness of Monsieur Guillotin's beheading apparatus. And whether they liked it or not, those who were suspicious of Napoleon's political leanings were forced out of sheer necessity to reinstate him to military command in order to help fill this dangerous vacuum.

Napoleon would receive several assignments in the next year, but being run ragged all over the French countryside with ill-defined objectives, and with a very-ill equipped military, proved to be bad for his health. Under these poor conditions he managed to contract malaria, an illness that would come to plague him for the rest of his life. However, sickness aside, Napoleon trudged on and once he recovered he would find his chance to endear himself with the ruling authority of the National Assembly.

It was on October 5th 1795 that Napoleon found himself rescuing General Paul Barras, the head of the Directory, by deploying artillery pieces near the palace and having his men fire on the counterrevolutionaries, crushing their short lived rebellion against the assembly. As a result Napoleon had once again gained the status of "hero;" as this time he was viewed as heroic from the more politically expedient side of the French Revolution, he was finally able to capitalize on his patriotic gains.

His new political benefactors were very generous. In their gratitude they awarded Napoleon a place as Commander of the Army of the Interior. It was in this role that he was instructed to disarm Paris after it had suffered through the counterrevolutionary riots. In an attempt to keep the peace, an edict had been issued that no private citizen should have any weapon in their house. Tired of the turmoil, most Parisians readily agreed to this forced disarmament, but one young man by the name of Eugene De Beauharnais was not very happy about the situation.

After his deceased father's sword had been taken from his home, De Beauharnais tracked down General Napoleon himself in order to demand its return. During this dramatic confrontation the young Eugene threatened to commit suicide if he was not returned his father's sword; Napoleon was supposedly moved with compassion for the young man and granted his request.

This then prompted Eugene's mother Josephine to pay a visit to thank the General for his generosity. It was due to the very same reign of terror that had just killed Robespierre and briefly imprisoned Napoleon that Josephine had been recently widowed. Her husband Alexander, the orphaned Eugene's father, had fallen on the wrong side of the Revolution like so many others before him and had met his fate on the French Guillotine.

It was Napoleon Bonaparte that would soon become this widow of the Revolution's new husband; the two married on March 9th, 1796. By all accounts Napoleon was madly in love with his new bride, but their honeymoon was short lived. Just a few days after their wedding the Little Corporal would be called to battle anew, and the "Little Corporal" would find himself taking charge once again.

Chapter One

Napoleon Takes Charge

The newly wed Napoleon went on the offensive in Italy. In a rapid fire burst of victorious routs and sieges he knocked the forces of Piedmont out of the war in a matter of weeks. Piedmont, an area that basically encompassed northwest Italy, shared a border with France; surrounded by the Alps, it had been a contested piece of European real estate for many years.

The French had for some time set their sights upon making Piedmont, long under the dominion of Austria, their own client state. In 1796 Napoleon Bonaparte seemed like just the man to finally accomplish this dream. The only problem was his ill-equipped and half starved army of 38,000 men—an army that was already on its last legs, as it soldiers suffered from severe battle fatigue from the last four years of intermittent skirmishes they had faced on the southern slopes of the Alps.

However, Napoleon was a charismatic commander. It is said that he had an incredible ability to move his weary, half-starved men to action. In one supposed discourse from the general, he told them, "soldiers, you are insufficiently clothed, malnourished; the government owes you much but is unable to repay anything. I wish to lead you into the most fertile valleys of the world. Wealthy regions, large cities will be under your power. You will find in those parts honor, glory, and riches."

This speech helped Napoleon galvanize his exhausted group of Frenchmen, lead them through the Alps, and on to victory in northern Italy. The first battle of this campaign took place on April 12th 1796 against a force of 56,000. Napoleon's rag-tag band was able to inflict over 3000 casualties. In just a matter of weeks the French had managed to completely overrun their enemy and force the ruling entity of their opponent, King Victor the Third, to the negotiating table.

About one year later on the heels of a spectacular victory that left 14,000 more Austrians dead, Napoleon was at the gates of Vienna itself. In April, almost one year to the day of King Victor's defeat, the Emperor of the Holy Roman Empire—the major power broker of central Europe of which Austria was the seat—was forced to ask Napoleon for terms of peace. After a humiliating defeat Emperor Francis was forced to sign the "Treaty of Campo Formio", significantly diminishing the empire by cutting off Lombardy and the entire left bank of the Rhine.

With his enemies in central Europe defeated, Napoleon turned his attention to his adversary to the northwest: Great Britain. After receiving word of Austria's defeat the British were determined to stop Napoleon and wished very much to engage the French directly. However, Napoleon wasn't going to fall for that trap; being the wise strategist that he was, he realized that even he couldn't stand up to the full onslaught of the British Navy.

Since he was not yet prepared to strike at England itself, he chose the next best thing: he hatched a plan to deal a death blow to the British economy by seizing Egypt and disrupting British commerce with its most valuable resource - India. The idea was to significantly diminish Britain's wealth and power by cutting off access to its colonial powerhouse while at the same enriching France's own coffers with the resources of Egypt and strengthening its foothold in the Mediterranean.

It was amazing that the government of France ever agreed to such a grandiose mission in the first place, but since the days of the French Revolution, this was the sentiment of the times. Couple this burst of national audaciousness with Napoleon Bonaparte and suddenly anything was possible. Napoleon's mission in Egypt was not just a military campaign, though; he also sought to score points on the diplomatic front.

Egypt had been territory of the Turkish Ottoman Empire for hundreds of years, yet it had fallen into decline through the recent decades and had all but broken away from the Ottomans. A land that had suffered through conquest for thousands of years, Egypt's most recent overlords were the Mamelukes, Muslim warlords who had ripped Egypt out of the Ottoman orbit. Amazingly, Napoleon surmised that getting rid of the Ottoman Sultan's rivals in Egypt would actually be doing the Ottoman Empire a favor, and that he would be seen as aiding the Sultan by making the Egyptian province once again toe the line.

The Sultan of course did not view French troops laying siege of Egypt as a favor no matter what good will Napoleon tried to demonstrate. As soon as French soldiers set foot on Egyptian soil, the Ottoman Empire officially declared war. Despite the Sultan's fury however, by all accounts the French occupation of Egypt was rather benign – an occupation that could be considered one of the first Western forays into nation building in the Middle-East.

Napoleon tried to ensure the Egyptian population that he was not their conqueror but their liberator, freeing them from the tyranny of their old social order just as the French had been delivered from the bourgeoisie. To aid in his liberation propaganda, Napoleon even had his troops hand out tracts printed in Arabic that carried his own personal message, proclaiming, "People of Egypt. I come to restore your rights, to punish the usurpers; I respect God, his prophet and the Quran more than did the Mamelukes. We are the friends of all true Muslims."

However, most of the Egyptians weren't buying it. No matter what Napoleon tried to claim, the French were nothing more than infidel invaders that needed to be expelled at all cost in the eyes of the Egyptians. Rather than capitulate when Napoleon's men reached the walls of Alexandria, the entire city came to life in fierce resistance. Defenders mounted the parapet and took positions in towers with their muskets, raining down an endless barrage of fire on Napoleon's army.

However, the defenders and their low-grade, outdated muskets were no match for Napoleon's crack artillery unit. When Napoleon's canons began pounding the walls of Alexandria, the city pushed to its breaking point. In one last hope to drive Napoleon out, Ottoman cavalry converged on the scene and began charging the French artillery. Napoleon's troops proved that they were more than ready for such an attack; they positioned themselves in defensive square formations that the Ottomans were unable to break.

Every time the cavalry charged one of these square units, Napoleon's men held their ground, unleashing a fusillade of gunfire. Any Egyptian cavalry that managed to get through this withering blast were quickly skewered with the long pikes affixed as bayonets to the specialized French rifles. Soon, Napoleon found himself successfully rolling across Egypt.

This was not a situation that the other powers in Europe could permit to happen – especially England. Although the British fleet had let Napoleon slip through their grasp during his initial invasion of Egypt, the British captain Horatio Nelson caught up with the French fleet in Alexandria and blew it to pieces. It was an all-out devastating loss for the French in which only two ships out of thirteen managed to escape.

However, even worse than the loss of ships, the attack left Napoleon virtually abandoned in Egypt with all access to France completely cut off. As resourceful as he was, Napoleon decided that he would make the best of it and began to fancy himself Emperor of Egypt. Even though he and his small army were surrounded in a sea of completely hostile enemies, as bleak as the situation was his confidence didn't seem to waver.

Neither did his mother's for that matter. While friends and family back home began to fear the worst for Napoleon, his mother is recorded as saying, "My son will not die in Egypt as his enemies are hoping. I know that a higher destiny lies before him." Confidence and a trust in fate seemed to run rampant in the whole Bonaparte family tree, but both mother and son were correct in their assessment of the situation. Despite the odds, Napoleon ultimately escaped the whole affair unscathed and arrived back in France on October 1799 to claim his throne.

Chapter Two

The Napoleonic Code

When Napoleon returned from his Egyptian campaign, France was once again in political turmoil. Despite the chaos, the soldier class in Paris remained fiercely loyal to Napoleon; when it was suggested that he lead a coup d'état against the Directory that governed France, the military pledged its full support. However, when Napoleon stood up before Council of Ancients (as the French political body was known as) to request status as a consulate in place of the Directory, he nearly lost his nerve.

It seems that Napoleon, a general and commander who was used to issuing orders to disciplined military men who followed his every word without question for years, had forgotten what it was like to deal with unruly and defiant politicians. When he attempted to give his speech before the council, they didn't care what he had to say; Napoleon, who was used to being adored by his unquestioning underlings, was now being rudely shouted down with cries of, "Down with the Tyrant! Down with the dictator! Outlaw him!"

Who knows if the rabid crowd really did sense the threat of an impending Napoleonic dictatorship. However, in this raucous moment they called the shots, and for once a bewildered Napoleon didn't know what to do. As he became paralyzed with fear, the belligerent crowd got even uglier as one of the nearby deputies trumped the verbal abuse by actually reaching over and striking the shell-shocked Napoleon across the face. This disheveled and subdued image of Bonaparte is one that we are used to seeing.

Things got even more out of control when someone else in the crowd pulled a gun and waved it right in Bonaparte's face - a bizarre turn of events for a man that had just led a showdown against the Ottoman Empire and lived to tell the tale. Obviously rattled by the aggression, Napoleon was forced to beat a hasty retreat outside of the building. There he finally managed to requisition some of his troops for support against the hostile mob. The troublemakers were eventually forced to leave and the remaining Council members took a vote without them, appointing Napoleon to the position.

Upon his appointment to the Consulate, Napoleon famously declared, "We have finished the romance of the Revolution. We must now begin its history, only seeking what is real and practicable in the application of its principles, and not what is speculative and hypothetical." This was Napoleon's signatory sign off that marked the final end of the French Revolution and the beginning of the Napoleonic reign.

However, on the eve of his coronation there were tidings of war once again in northern Italy. Napoleon had to send his soldiers to put down an uprising in Piedmont. Napoleon was ultimately triumphant however; after the Austrian's defeat at Marengo in 1800 he consolidated his gains into an enlarged Cisalpine Republic. Napoleon then went about creating his own Italian defense force that would be loyal to him and work to further safeguard his interests in the area.

As well as working to consolidate his military hold, Napoleon also worked to consolidate his political grasp of the Italian people. Just as he tried to do in Egypt when he claimed he was freeing native Egyptians from the tyranny of the Mamelukes, Napoleon once again attempted to present himself as a liberator. He informed the local Italians that he was liberating them from the Austrians and other foreign enemies who wished to snuff out their heritage and way of life.

At the Consulte of Lyon he declared to them, "Invaded by enemy armies, your existence appeared no longer possible, when the people of France, for a second time, chased by force of arms, your enemies from your land." However, Napoleon knew that words alone wouldn't work to convince the locals of his sincerity, he needed a powerful political ally - for this the only logical counterpart would be the Pope.

In July 1801 an official concordat was reached with Pope Pius VII in which the Pope accepted that Napoleon would appoint French bishops and that church lands that were seized during the revolution would not be restored. In return for the Pope's acceptance of these terms, Napoleon agreed to pay a generous salary to the clergy and to recognize Catholicism as the major religion of the region.

For the first time since the Revolution, Napoleon had restored the Catholic Church in France and by virtue of this restoration he had given himself a badge of tremendous legitimacy among the Italians. It was as if Napoleon was recreating the Carolingian Empire and like Charlemagne was suddenly viewed as a defender of the Christian faith. In reality the relationship was purely political. Napoleon, who had previously professed himself a deist, was not that interested in Christianity; however the alliance served his purpose nonetheless.

By way of Napoleon's strategic advances on both the military and the political front he managed to broker peace and by 1802, the Treaty of Amiens made sure that he was no longer fighting with Austria, England or anyone else. It was the first time that France had been at peace since 1792. Napoleon then followed up this peace on the international front by attempting to make the political climate of his own country more favorable, beginning with his declaration of general amnesty on April 26 1802 which allowed all but the "most notorious" émigrés and political dissidents to return to France.

It was with his reconciliation with the Catholic Church and his signing of general amnesty that Napoleon managed to help to finally bring calm to the areas of French society that had been afflicted the worst by the Revolution. With these two major obstacles out of his way, Napoleon then spent the rest of his energy undertaking a wide variety of civic reforms, in what was widely known as his Napoleonic Code, as an attempt to stabilize his Empire.

The Napoleonic Code would reform everything from the banking system to which side of the road his citizens would travel on, with the latter enabling two-way traffic on city streets for the first time. In fact it is due to Napoleonic reform that most of us drive on the right side of the road to this day. It was also at this time that Napoleon sold France's Louisiana Territory—the only remaining French outpost in the New World—to the United States in what would become known as the Louisiana Purchase.

He sold the property to Thomas Jefferson for a reported 80 million francs, a much needed dividend in the depleted coffers of France. The generation of this income is said to have helped to sustain Napoleon's massive army for the next ten years. Napoleon additionally justified his sale of Louisiana on the grounds that a strong America would only benefit the French; he is quoted as saying at the time of the sale, "It is in the interest of France that America be strong".

Napoleon's civil codes did much to enhance and better the lives of a French citizenry. As a result it was unanimously decided to name Napoleon "First Consul for life" in 1802. Shortly after this declaration, Napoleon's international peace would break apart; in 1803, Britain would once again wage war against France. Russia and Austria would do likewise in turn. It was in the backdrop of this new outbreak of unrest, just as the bullets were beginning to fly anew, that the French Senate proclaimed Napoleon Bonaparte to be their Emperor.

Chapter Three

On the Road to Empire

When Napoleon was crowned emperor on May 18th 1804, his was an empire at war. The British remained the driving force of opposition with their resistance to the French Empire beginning in earnest in 1803 when British ships began seizing French merchant vessels. Under the Treaty of Amiens this was viewed as an instance somewhat akin to piracy; Napoleon made his displeasure known. In an act of swift retaliation the French began to immediately seize British goods and to detain British subjects.

It is reported that almost all British males between the ages of 18 and 60 in France were arrested, something that disrupted many families in the region. Napoleon viewed this seizure as a rightful retaliation; the rest of the world of course viewed these draconian measures as a sure sign of Napoleon Bonaparte's tyranny being implemented on a global scale. With no excuse to play by the rules any more, the British ripped their copy of the Treaty of Amiens to shreds and began a renewed all-out war against the French.

In the ensuing conflict, Napoleon again realized that there was no way to defeat the immense naval power of Britain on the high seas. A plan for a land invasion was necessary; Bonaparte's administration knew clearly well that although Britain was a giant on the sea they were weak on land with an army that numbered less than one hundred thousand regulars. If only Napoleon could get his superior land forces onto British soil, his victory seemed almost certain. Invasion plans were drawn up accordingly in order to maximize the French infantry's strength.

In staging this mass exodus of French infantry into the British homeland Napoleon quickly realized that in order for any land invasion to work he must gain complete control of the English Channel. He had to have complete dominance over this waterway so that the British Navy would be unable to disrupt his invasion flotilla. Without this assurance, the size of his invasion force would be irrelevant if the British fleet was able to pick off every member of his "grand armeé" as they attempted to set foot on the shoreline.

In order to make sure that the Channel would stay under his control, Napoleon concocted a plan to team up with his allied Spanish fleets in the Mediterranean and then use this combined force to break through the British Navy stationed in the English Channel. At the first outset of the struggle however, Admiral Villeneuve, the commander of the Spanish fleet, seemed to lose his nerve; after an initial confrontation with Horatio Nelson's British fleet, Villeneuve sailed his forces back to Spain.

Initially this seemed to work in Napoleon's favor, as a large contingent of Nelson's navy left the English Chanel to actively pursue the Spanish fleet. This left the Channel's own naval protection drastically reduced. Meanwhile, Napoleon's own intelligence reports seemed to confirm that six main British ships were docked in Gibraltar off the southern shores of Spain.

Perceiving an opportunity to strike, Napoleon galvanized his resolve and committed his remaining forces to engage the British fleet in the Channel. Additionally, Admiral Villenueve canceled his retreat, ordering his own forces to join up with Napoleon's. The combined Franco-Spanish armada is said to have stretched out five miles long as Nelson's fleet came near. The battle soon turned into a swirling chaos of cannon fire without any immediate sign of who would gain the other hand.

Finally, in one dramatic instance in the middle of the chaos the British ship Victory managed to lock masts with the French vessel Redoutable. This action would prove to be a bit misguided for the British and ultimately fatal for their commander, Horratio Nelson. The crew of the Redoubtable contained a crack unit of French infantry and sharpshooters.

As soon as these two ships locked the French were more than ready to attempt to board and take over the British ship. However, a sharpshooter on the mizzentop of the Redoubtable showed mettle by dealing Horatio Nelson a deadly blow, firing a musket ball right through his left shoulder, and shattering his spine. The bullet finally came to rest in Nelson's right scapula. As soon as he was hit, the legendary war veteran could be heard exclaiming, "They finally succeeded, I am dead!"

However, Nelson didn't die instantly. As the battle raged, his wounded form could be seen hurriedly being carried below decks. At this point, due to French grenades being thrown at them and the threat of the French infantry boarding the ship, the Victory's gunners stopped firing and rushed to the deck of the ship. As bleak as things may have seemed however, the beleaguered ship's salvation seemed to be on the horizon when the British freighter Temeraire joined the meleé.

In the midst of their attempts to storm the deck of the Victory, the French crew was caught off guard as the Temerarie began to fire mercilessly at their exposed positions on the deck of their ship. This bombardment directly into the crowd of the unsheltered French infantry resulted in many casualties, and of the 643 member crew, only 99 men were said to be left fully intact; the rest were either dead or severely wounded. Among the maimed and wounded from the explosive fury of the Temararie was the French ship's own captain who issued a quick and unconditional surrender.

The battle continued on with several more instances of French ships being overwhelmed in the same fashion until the Franco-Spanish fleet that was meant to be the invasion force of England was finally repulsed and defeated. It is said that as the wounded Horatio Nelson lay dying he approved of the British victory of Trafalgar - his dying words were to tell his subordinates, "Thank God I have done my duty." The Battle of Trafalgar would signal the end of Napoleon's challenge to Britain's naval power and would cause him to once again turn his eyes toward war with continental Europe.

Chapter Four

A Continent Under Siege

Napoleon's plans for an invasion of Britain were scuttled in the aftermath of Trafalgar. However, even though his war on the high seas was drawing to a close his battle over the lands of continental Europe were just beginning. Napoleon's first directive after the battle with the British was to impose a continental blockade over all the European states under his dominion, with the intent of weakening an already sputtering British economy.

Unable to strike at the British militarily, Napoleon once again turned to a strategy of hurting them economically by putting a stranglehold on all British commerce in continental Europe. Meanwhile on the military front Napoleon turned the majority of his forces toward Austria and managed to catch the Austrian General Mack completely by surprise by the rapid advance of the French infantry on Austrian borders.

It was here that the French would score a massive victory in this first leg of the new Austrian campaign at the Battle of Ulm. From here, Napoleon's army marched all the way to Vienna and occupied the Austrian capital by November. A counterattack was soon launched by a combined unit of Austrian and Russian forces. This allied group of fighters greatly outnumbered Napoleon's army and French defeat seemed imminent.

In one of the greatest military strategies of all time, Napoleon actually feigned defeat and pretended that his military was on the verge of collapse in order to lure the Austro-Russian forces into a trap. Napoleon even went so far as to send one of his Generals to meet with the Russians in order to supposedly broker a peace deal. This General was doing more than feeling for prospective peace terms; instead his presence was used to gather intelligence on the Russian defenses.

Napoleon's peace envoy resulted in a temporary armistice, which gave him more time to organize his forces. Napoleon then directed his troops to make a hasty retreat back from the front lines in order to lure the Austro-Russian army to follow them.

In one of the most masterful - if not outright mischievous - military strategies in history, Napoleon's forces crossed the frozen river fords of Austerlitz only to stop their march, position artillery, and then engage in a withering burst of artillery fire at the advancing enemy troops and even at the river itself. In one of the most disastrous military engagements of all time, the Austro-Russian forces fell through the thin ice, leaving a large chunk of the unit to drown with dozens of Russian artillery pieces sinking right alongside them.

This battle was a horrible blow to the allied war effort against Napoleon. A defeated and demoralized Austria signed the Treaty of Pressburg on December 4th; as a result the political entity of central Europe that was known as the Holy Roman Empire essentially ceased to exist. A powerhouse of the region was no more and Napoleon was once again supreme.

The following year would see Napoleon consolidate his foothold in central Europe by creating the "Confederation of the Rhine," a collective of German states that he instituted in order to create a buffer between France and Prussia. These moves encroached directly on Prussia's border. As the Prussians could not take such transgressions lightly, they declared war against France in 1806.

Prussian King Frederick-Wilhem II had issued a direct ultimatum to Napoleon, demanding that he either withdraw his army back behind the Rhine or to face the full might of the Prussian armed forces. The Prussians at this time boasted one of the most formidable militaries in Europe; most would think twice before challenging it. However, Napoleon's only response to this ultimatum was to send his military directly into the arms of the Prussian military machine, rapidly unleashing the full extent of French forces east of the Rhine. In an effort to launch a coordinated preemptive attack Napoleon then marched three parallel columns through the forests of Thuringia followed by a rapid thrust through the Salle valley, effectively cutting off the Prussian army's access to their line of communications in Berlin.

The opening battle on October 6th saw a Prussian division routed; this was then followed up by additional Prussian forces being obliterated in the German town of Saalfeld. With these early victories the momentum of the French army continued to build, eventually leading to the unheard-of defeat of the main Prussian army at the hands of just one single unit of French auxiliary corps at the Battle of Auerstedt.

In the initial onslaught Napoleon's army proved to do fairly well, managing to overrun many of the enemy garrisons before actually engaging the main Prussian force. With a string of amazing victories behind him, Napoleon and his army entered the city of Berlin on October 27th 1806. Despite his astonishing domination over the Germanic and Prussian forces that dared to stand against him, it is said that Napoleon did manage to display a small vestige of humility.

If accounts of the French army are to be believed, in Berlin Napoleon supposedly took the time to visit the tomb of another powerful leader, Fredrick the Great, informing his men that "if he were alive we wouldn't be here today." Napoleon's assessment may have been right; the Prussian and German forces that he faced were just a dwindling fraction of what they had been in their glory days under Fredrick, a dwindling power that resulted in Napoleon Bonaparte creating his own "Continental System" by official decree on November 21st, 1806, a system that grew to include Poland by June 14th, 1807, making Napoleon's imperial expansion for the French even greater than Charlemagne's was nearly 1000 years before. With these gains, Napoleon's hegemonic status over the continent seemed to be just about complete.

Chapter Five

Backroom Deals and the Division of Empire

After Napoleon's latest victories in central Europe, he was riding high. After the Russian army had been annihilated, Napoleon's men had set up camp right outside the Russian outpost of Tilsit, a strategic location situated right between Prussian and Russian territory in Poland. The war had taken its toll on the enemies of Napoleon and at this point even the mighty Russian bear was on its knees and ready to engage in peace talks with Bonaparte. So it was that Tsar Alexander sent an envoy to Napoleon's camp with the message that peace between Russia and France was needed in order to "ensure the happiness of the world."

From epic battle to epic peace agreement, these two men had their first face to face meeting on June 25th 1807. During this meeting Alexander supposedly told Napoleon, "Sire, I hate the English no less than you do and I am ready to assist you in any enterprise against them." Apparently this was music to Napoleon's ears; at the mention of Russia taking a stance of antagonism against France's arch-nemesis, the two quickly began to hammer out their terms of peace.

The peace deal had many twists, turns and idiosyncrasies, but among these, probably the most comical was the fact that Napoleon made sure to make a special request to Alexander to have the Russian Orthodox Church rescind its proclamation that Napoleon was the antichrist. Not a religious man himself, yet still wanting to fare well in the prophetic beliefs of others, Napoleon never ceased in his desire to rule the hearts and minds of those he was engaged with.

The treaty with the Russians was finalized on July 7th to be followed by a similar peace with Prussia two days later. This brought both of these European powerhouses within Napoleon's Continental System that forbade them to trade with England. The next two years that followed would see great political intrigue both internationally and the home front, including the very home of Napoleon himself.

In 1809 the Bonaparte household was awash in rumors of an impending divorce between Napoleon and Josephine, his wife of over a decade. These rumors came to a head on December 15th of that year when Napoleon forced a weeping Josephine to read a speech that declared the dissolution of their marriage on the grounds that she was unable to bear him children. In the midst of the tears of a former Empress, the clerical tribunal officially annulled the marriage of the Bonapartes.

This dissolved marriage was then replaced by what Napoleon hoped would be a more palpable one for his royal ambition in the form of the Arch Duchess Maria Louisa of Austria, whom he married in March of 1810. Maria's father was the Emperor of Austria, and by means of this marriage Napoleon sought to establish a dynastic bond with his old rival. As an added bonus (or So Napoleon thought) Maria's aunt happened to be none other than the not-so long ago guillotined Marie Antoinette.

Napoleon had always been a bit insecure about his upbringing, likely not helped by schoolyard taunts against his Corsican heritage. He was laboring under the erroneous impression that being somehow connected to the old royal blood of France would give his own rule more legitimacy. However, bringing back the specter of the deposed royal family would mostly serve to revive all of the old jealousies and resentments the French had for the royals before the revolution even began.

Meanwhile, as Napoleon played bridegroom, the economy of his recently pacified Russia began to stall. Looking for a solution, the same Tsar who had once professed his hatred of the British to Napoleon began to once again open up his ports to British merchants. This of course did not sit well with Bonaparte; considering this a clear violation of their treaty; Napoleon launched a new invasion centered squarely on Russia in 1812.

The invasion force that Napoleon unleashed was massive, consisting of 600,000 French, Dutch, Prussian, Polish, and Austrian soldiers - the largest coalition that he had ever assembled. This new "grand armeé" crossed over the Neman River and into the lands of Russia on June 22nd, 1812. At first Napoleon's forces easily slammed through the Russian outskirts with next to no resistance. The only fighting force they encountered was a group of Cossacks who, upon estimating the size of Napoleon's force, fled in terror. In the first few days of Napoleon's campaign, resistance remained minimal.

Russian reinforcements were also further delayed by the direction of General Barclay, the man in charge of the main Russian contingent. Instead of engaging Napoleon directly, Barclay took refuge in Moscow in an attempt to organize a larger army to send after the French. Tsar Alexander soon grew impatient of this cat and mouse game; unhappy with Barclay's strategy, the Tsar had him replaced with the more experienced Mikhail Kutuzov, who adopted a more aggressive strategy.

Kutuzov, a veteran of Austerlitz, sought to repay Napoleon the favor of what he had done to the Russian army by luring him into a trap. The idea was to lure Napoleon's army out into the open heartland of Russia, stretching Bonaparte's forces too thin while partisans implementing guerilla warfare tactics slowly ate away at his army. Kutuzov also made sure to implement an infamous "scorched earth" policy, torching every town right before it was lost to Napoleon so that he and his men would not be able to gain any use from it, resulting in the destruction of a huge chunk of mainland Russia just to deprive the French of supplies.

This wanton destruction was the most devastating to Russian farmers and peasants, leading to many abandoning their country in favor of the French, joining ranks with Napoleon out of their own rage over their government's callousness. It seemed like pure insanity that the Russian authority was willing to destroy its own country, but the scorched earth policy remained in place, even when it came to the very heart of Russian civilization: as soon as Napoleon reached Moscow, it was in flames.

The French army entered the flaming inferno that used to be the Russian capital on September 13th, 1812. Napoleon quickly moved to regain a vestige of order from the chaos and worked to establish a military government over the destroyed city. At this point, Mikhail Kutuzov and his army were long gone, seeking higher ground in the East preparing for their final stand. Napoleon, taking their departure as a sign of defeat, set up camp in Moscow thinking that Tsar Alexander would be contacting him for peace talks and the making of another treaty.

But no treaty ever came. Napoleon realized that he would have to track down the phantom army that the Russian military had become. In his haste, he left the city of Moscow barely defended with 5000 severely wounded soldiers laid up in the city's hospital. Napoleon was hoping that there would be no more need to protect a burned-out city and a few thousand wounded men, but he was wrong; as soon as Napoleon's main army left Moscow, Russian partisans slipped back into the city and massacred all 5000 of Napoleon's recovering soldiers. They then burned what was left of the city completely to the ground.

By the time Napoleon finally managed to engage the reorganized Russian army on October 19th, his own military had rapidly deteriorated from starvation and the elements of an already cold Russian winter. Battered and defeated, Napoleon's army was repelled and forced to make a retreat. As his men made their grand escape, it was a disaster. Even when they managed to evade the fire of the main Russian force, the French army was mercilessly hounded by Cossacks and other partisans through the countryside while simultaneously succumbing to hunger and subzero temperatures.

By late November, what remained Napoleon's army reached French occupied Lithuania and the battle against the Russians was all but lost. In December, after hearing word of rumors of his demise and a possible coup in Paris, Napoleon was forced to abandon what was left of his fighting force and head back to France. He arrived back to the heart of his kingdom on December 18th.

To his horror, Napoleon would later learn that he had lost over 400,000 men in the Russian campaign without even fully engaging the enemy. Rather than being defeated in battle, Napoleon's military was mainly defeated by the Russian winter and lack of supplies. The biting frost and howling wind served as the backdrop for the sad conclusion of Napoleon Bonaparte's imperial aspirations.

Chapter Six

Exile and the Napoleonic Last Stand

On October 16th 1813, Napoleon found himself staring down a fighting force of over one million troops that were setting a collision course for his own meager force of 200,000 soldiers. For most people the situation would have seemed absolutely hopeless, but Napoleon, never one to admit defeat, fought on. Two days later he would be defeated, with anti-Napoleonic forces controlling all of France. Napoleon officially abdicated the throne on April 4th, 1814.

As terms of his surrender, Napoleon agreed to go into a self imposed exile on the island of Elba. He left peacefully but not without a few cryptically chosen parting words; he told the French people, "I would embrace every one of you to display my affection, but I will kiss this flag, for it represents all of you. But you know that I shall return to France when the violets will bloom." Many would later view these words as prophetic as Napoleon would escape his captivity in Elba beyond all odds and return to the French mainland the following spring.

For the French, spring couldn't come soon enough. To just about every French citizen's dismay, after Napoleon's abdication, the plans for regime change orchestrated by the European powers meant an attempt to reinstate the French monarchy by placing Louis XVIII on the throne in Napoleon's place. This could not have been a more unpopular thing to do; as a result, riots in Paris became quite commonplace. Secret organizations began to spring up on every corner with only one obsessive objective in mind - bringing Napoleon Bonaparte back to power.

These were certainly welcome sentiments to a miserable Napoleon. Even though his abdication was a peaceful effort of his own volition, by all accounts he was a broken man. There is even mention that he attempted to commit suicide during his first few days on Elba. Napoleon, being the headstrong person he was, eventually managed to banish these misgivings, shove down the pangs of depression and despair, and focus on how he could reassert himself on the world stage.

Ironically, according to the agreement of his abdication from France he was still able to retain the title of Emperor; the jurisdiction of his empire had just been reduced to the tiny island of Elba. Controlling a mere 12,000 inhabitants, Napoleon tried to make the best of his miniature kingdom, reforming the civil code and creating a rudimentary military. In Napoleon's mind, he probably began to view his exile as just a temporary setback, as he sought to hatch his next grand scheme.

This "Island Emperor" had become a bit of a joke with many of his former European colleagues. However, the wiser thinking heads of the coalition weren't ready to take any more chances and sought to take even Napoleon's dominion of Elba away from him, seeking a more permanent solution to the troublemaking Bonaparte by shipping him off to an even more remote island in the Atlantic for a more permanent exile. When Napoleon learned of this plan, he immediately determined to make his escape. Gathering up 1050 men from the island, Bonaparte made a break for the French mainland, arriving on its shores two days later.

Bonaparte was immediately intercepted by the French infantry. However, rather than arresting him, they welcomed him back as their Emperor and proceeded to reinstate him to the throne. Napoleon triumphantly stormed into Paris on March 19th 1815. This began the period known as "The Hundred Days," a period in which Napoleon rapidly reorganized French society and its military within just a few months.

In this timeframe, he managed to swell his military ranks with 200,000 volunteers from loyal veterans of his previous campaigns along with some new additions from Italy and Switzerland. The outpouring of support for Napoleon was an incredible triumph for the Emperor and a baffling thorn in the side of the Coalition that sought to shut him down. Napoleon, as pragmatic as ever, knew that his country was not ready for another conflict; he tried his best to negotiate a truce with the other European powers, but his European neighbors weren't interested. The Coalition saw blood, and like sharks in the water, were ready to strike down the floundering Bonaparte's weakened empire.

Seeing that a short term peace deal was not possible, Napoleon decided it was either all or nothing. He marched his men on the offensive over the border of Belgium in an attempt to divide the British and Prussian forces that were advancing on him. In one more stunning victory at the Battle of Ligny, Napoleon managed to crush the Prussian force on June 16th and at the same time caused the British army to fall back.

In the aftermath of yet another Napoleonic military miracle, many held their breath wondering if somehow Bonaparte could pull off the impossible, coming out of exile with a greatly outnumbered fighting force and somehow defeat the allied coalition. But then came Waterloo - a name that has become synonymous with complete and utter defeat.

The Battle of Waterloo occurred on June 18th, 1815, and proved to be Napoleon's final engagement from which he would never recover. The day before this watershed military engagement, all fighting had been delayed from torrential rainfall stalling all military operations in the area. The excessive moisture had managed to cripple both the French and British artillery.

However, the next day saw the French cavalry gaining the initial advantage, pushing the British back, only to be stymied by Prussian reinforcements whose massive offensive obliterated the entire right wing of Napoleon's army. Napoleon's soldiers knew all too well that the battle was lost; and in one last act of loyalty to their Emperor they formed a protective square around Napoleon, giving Bonaparte enough time to escape as they fought to the death.

Napoleon fled back to Paris where, after considering the massive impending destruction that loomed over the city, admitted his defeat. Once again he stepped down from the throne. Napoleon wished to spare his people from needless destruction; at the same time he did not wish to be exiled to a lonely island. Before the British arrived he attempted yet another daring escape, placing his bets on the United States of all places, where he hoped to be granted exile.

However, Napoleon's intents to live out his own version of the American dream were quickly dashed when the British finally laid their hands on him in the British blockade of Rochefort on July 3rd 1815. After grabbing up the former Emperor they then wasted no time to place him at his new home of permanent exile on the island of St. Helena.

On this remote little piece of real estate in the Atlantic, Napoleon spent his final days playing cards, writing his memoirs and ruminating about the past to anyone that would listen to him. Finally, he succumbed to his most deadly foe of all, the stomach cancer that took his life on May 5th 1821.

Conclusion

Everyone Wants to Rule the World

After France's acquisition of Corsica, Napoleon's father Carlo placed the young Napoleon in military school, at the time the fast track to a good career. But as a youth Napoleon seemed more interested in his books than military adventures. When Napoleon was a child he was noted as being very studious and his grades in school would later reflect a man who was quite an intellectual. If circumstances were different he could have pursued an entirely different path in life. But it was through the unknown and capricious whims of fate that he found himself an Artillery captain, a general, and then ultimately an emperor.

It is often argued that Napoleon was a megalomaniac and narcissist, full of himself and his own selfish desire to rule the world. But we are all a product of our experiences in life, and we shape our mindset as we grow. Napoleon was a child of the Revolution and his mindset was shaped as such. He was abruptly uprooted from his Corsican home as a child and sent to a land completely unknown where he was expected to prove himself as a man.

He then entered into adolescence and the added anxiety of his precarious social situation served to reinforce something we all go through as a teenager - that ever so intangible desire "to be somebody". The often expressed desire to be famous, well liked, successful; these are all strong desires that scream at the teenage mind. At the tender age of just 16, with these perfectly normal teenage delusions of grandeur filling his brain, Napoleon was then thrust into a major conflict that gave him that chance live out this fantasy: finally he was someone important. He could command success. For him the adolescent dream became reality, and he acquired a sufficiently inflated ego to match.

The social devastation of the French Revolution then further allowed egos such as Napoleon's to insert themselves in what would have been ordinarily inaccessible positions. This was the perfect storm and recipe for the enlightened despot. If Carlo had sent Napoleon off to be an attorney, a playwright, or a musician, we would most likely be singing a completely different tune.

27185457R00024

Made in the USA
Columbia, SC
19 September 2018